MONEY-UP

INVESTING FOR TEENS & YOUNG PEOPLE

Jojo star press

TABLE OF
CONTENTS

Introduction

01 Invest In Yourself Before the Toys

02 Become a Money Maker

03 Diversification is King

04 Stack the Stock

05   **Bond-Up**

06   **Ring REITs**

07   **Let's Get Mutual**

08   **Play ETFs**

09   **Commodity Zone**

10   Fomo Crypto

11   My Precious Collectibles

12   Market the Money

13   Manage Your Portfolio Youngsters

INTRODUCTION

If you don't have to worry about money, what will you do with your time? Will you tour the globe and experience it or will you choose to spend more time with the people you love? What are you going to do?

All of this can only be accomplished through financial independence, which can only be acquired by frequent and early investments.

Let's get one thing straight right now, young champ: you can't work nonstop. No matter how tough and powerful you are today as a youth, you will age, and you will need your investment to support your lifestyle.

Me personally, I began investing at the age of 17. I grew up with my Dad because my mother passed away when I was only 7 years old, and because he is an active duty member, I had to assume some financial responsibility.

I read anything I could get my hands on, including financial websites and books. I had to learn how to file taxes and began investing in stocks through brokers, but there have never been more accessible venues for you to invest now at the press of a button on your iPhone.

This book provides clear and simple-to-understand explanations of the basics of investing. The book covers a variety of topics, such as how to analyze financial statements, mutual funds, exchange-traded funds, equities, and how to create a portfolio and more.

It also provides advice on smart financial strategies including diversification, long-term investing, and risk management.

Additionally, it provides advice on how to handle tax liabilities, market volatility, and other monetary issues. To help young adults comprehend the concepts presented in the book, Investing for young people also includes a variety of case studies and real-world scenarios.

Chapter 1: Invest In Yourself Before the Toys

The ability to resist the allure of an immediate reward or pleasure in favor of a higher reward or benefit later on is known as "delayed gratification." One must be able to resist momentary temptations if they are to accomplish long-term goals.

This includes delaying the purchase of a new phone or device as long as the one you already own is still functional. The fundamental benefit of delaying gratification is that it fosters self-control and patience, two qualities that are essential for success.

Those who practice delayed gratification typically make better selections because they have the capacity to think about the long-term repercussions of their choices.

They have a higher propensity to save money for the future, make wise financial decisions, and resist the need to make impulsive purchases. Additionally, delaying pleasure might pave the way for future achievement.

People who postpone pleasure are better able to focus on their long-term goals and desires, which elevates their sense of accomplishment.

It is crucial that I make it clear that delaying gratification does not entail depriving yourself of life experiences. Visiting the movies or going on an adventure with friends that costs $100 shouldn't be put off because they are special moments that no amount of money can replace if neglected at your age.

It's okay to have fun with your friends while you're still young because as you get older and get more life experience, your earning potential will rise. However, it's crucial to know the difference between investing and saving.

Investing vs Saving

Saving and investing are both methods to spend money, but they serve distinct objectives.

Saving is the act of setting money away in a secure location, such a bank savings account, for future use. For instance,

if you save $100 in a bank account, you can utilize that money to purchase a future item that you'll desire or need.

Investing is the process of using money to purchase goods with the expectation that their value will rise, such as stocks, bonds, or real estate. For instance, if you invest $100 in a stock, its value might rise in the future, allowing you to sell it for more money.

A different approach to think about it is as follows: Savings refers to setting money aside for the short term, while investing refers to setting money away for the long term with the hope of generating more money in the future.

It's critical to keep in mind that investing always entails some risk, which means there is a potential you may lose all of your money. Contrarily, saving is typically viewed as a low-risk activity.

Thus, investing may be more ideal for those who are ready to accept increased risk in exchange for the possibility of greater returns, whilst saving may be more suitable for those who choose a more conservative approach.

Now that you are aware of the differences between saving and investing, let's examine the many sorts of investors that exist today. After all, as soon as you begin investing, you are an investor.

Types of Investors

There are several types of investors, each with its own unique approach to investing. Here are a few examples:

- **Value Investors**:These investors concentrate on identifying firms that are selling at a discount to their real worth and that the market has undervalued. They are certain that the market will eventually grasp the genuine worth of the business and the stock price will rise.

- **Growth Investors**: These investors concentrate on making investments in businesses with significant development potential, such as those operating in quickly expanding industries or offering novel goods or services. They think that these businesses will produce substantial profits in the future.

- **Income Investors**:These investors prioritize making money off of their investments, whether it be dividends or interest. They might put money into stocks, bonds, or other sources of income.

- **Index Investors**: These investors make investments in a portfolio of securities that resembles a market index, such the S&P 500. They think that by making investments in a variety of assets, they will get returns that are comparable to those of the market as a whole.

- **<u>Hedge Fund Investors</u>**: These investors make investments in hedge funds, which are pooled funds that make use of a variety of investing techniques, including short selling, leverage, and derivatives, to produce profits. They are frequently viewed as being more speculative and riskier than conventional investments.

- **<u>Momentum Investors</u>**: Due to their conviction that current performance will continue in the future, these investors concentrate on investing in assets that have done well recently.

- **<u>Contrarian Investors</u>**:These investors go against the grain by purchasing undervalued assets and offloading popular ones. They think that ultimately these assets will be appropriately valued because the market is frequently inefficient.

It's important to keep in mind that investors can be any one of these kinds or a combination of them, and that the precise investing plan that investor selects will rely on their personal objectives, risk tolerance, and time horizon.

Debunking some Investment Myths

Here are a few examples of common investment myths, along with explanations and why they are not true:

Myth: You can get rich quickly through investing.

FACT- Investment growth takes time since it is a long-term plan. While making a major return on investment fast is conceivable, it is not always a certainty, and many investments might take years to provide meaningful profits. Additionally, there is a considerable danger of loss associated with investments that promise rapid profits and are sometimes too good to be true.

Myth: You need a lot of money to start investing.

FACT- With just a few bucks, you can begin investing. It is simple to invest little sums of money and progressively expand your portfolio over time using a variety of online platforms and apps.

Myth: You need to be an expert to invest successfully.

FACT- You don't have to be an expert to start investing, even if it might be complicated. You may choose investments that fit your goals and risk tolerance by being knowledgeable about investing fundamentals, diversifying your portfolio, and, if you choose, consulting a financial counselor.

Myth: You should only invest in stocks that have gone up in the past.

FACT- The previous performance of a stock is not a guarantee that it will continue to rise. Future results cannot be predicted by past results. Before making an investment choice, it's critical to do your homework and take other aspects into account, such as the management of the company, its financial health, and market trends.

Myth: You should time the market to make the most money.

FACT- It may be very difficult and expensive to time the market. Many industry professionals think it's hard to accurately foresee market trends, and that attempting to do so might cost you opportunities for profit. Regular and long-term investment is a superior course of action.

Myth: You should only invest in what you know.

FACT- It's not essential to be an industry or sector specialist, but it's crucial to have a fundamental grasp of the investments you make. It is possible to lower risk and increase growth prospects by diversifying your portfolio by purchasing a range of assets.

Always conduct your own research before making an investing choice and avoid relying on rumors or unreliable sources.

<u>Common Types of Investment</u>

There are a variety of investments that you can learn about and comprehend; I'll mention them here with a brief explanation, but we'll look at them in more detail later on in this book. These investments include:

- **<u>Stock/Equity investments</u>**: A stake of ownership in a company is obtained by investing in its stock, which also offers the chance to profit from dividends and capital growth.

- **<u>Bond Investments</u>**: Investing in government- or company-issued debt securities with periodic interest payments and maturity principal returns.

- **<u>Real-Estate Investment Trust (REITs)</u>**: These are a particular class of investment vehicle that enables investors to buy a variety of income-producing real estate assets, including office buildings, malls, flats, and hotels. As with other equities, REITs are listed on stock exchanges and frequently distribute a sizable portion of their earnings as dividends to investors.

- **<u>Mutual Fund Investments</u>**:purchasing stocks, bonds, or other securities from a professionally managed portfolio.

- **Exchange-traded Fund (ETF) Investments**: investing in a portfolio of assets that tracks an industry or market index, such as the technology sector or the S&P 500.

- **Commodity Investments**: investing in tangible assets with the hope of profiting from price movements, such as agricultural products, precious metals, or oil.

- **Cryptocurrency Investments**: investing in digital currencies like Bitcoin or Ethereum with the hope of making money from their price growth.

- **Collectibles (e.g. art, stamps, coins)**: investing with the hope of profiting from an increase in value in goods like paintings, stamps, coins, and other collections.

- **Money Market Funds**: Investing in a portfolio of low-yielding but reasonably secure short-term debt instruments, including Treasury bills.

Chapter 2: Become a Money Maker

The ability to invest requires the ability to earn money while still a teen. Investing is a strategy to grow your money over time, but you need money to start investing.

Teenagers can earn money in a variety of ways, including through part-time employment, the launch of a small business, or even freelance labor.

Taking on a part-time job is one of the most popular methods for teenagers to earn money. Teenagers are frequently hired by businesses to work in fast food restaurants, as cashiers, or to stock shelves.

These professions not only give a means of support, but they also impart important life lessons like accountability, time management, and cooperation.

Teenagers might also establish a small company as a means of income. This may be everything from pet watching or dog walking to yard maintenance and snow removal to tutoring or computer help. An excellent approach to make money while learning about entrepreneurship and company management is by starting a small business.

Teenagers may generate money via freelancing as well. Writing, graphic design, social media management, and programming are a few examples of this. Teenagers who freelance can choose their own hours and select the tasks they wish to work on.

It's crucial that teens understand the value of money and smart money management. Making money while still a teen can assist them in building good credit, which will be crucial when they want to make future major purchases like a home or automobile.

I know it could seem like a challenging undertaking, but the main purpose is to find a career or start a small company that fits you. My first work was as a tutor, and I enjoyed it and it did help me save a lot of money.

 I will be more precise now and list out some common jobs and businesses, they include:

- Online Tutoring: There is a strong demand for online tutors across all subject areas because many students are now learning remotely as a result of the epidemic.

- Virtual assistance: Due to the fact that so many businesses today run entirely online, they frequently require help with activities like appointment setting, email replying, and social media management.

- Content creation: Users may produce, share, and monetize content on websites and apps like YouTube, TikTok, and Instagram.

- Online surveys and market research: Businesses are always seeking customer input on their goods and services, and often pay people to take part in focus groups and internet surveys.

- Online selling: Users may create an online store and sell their own goods or resale stuff they've already bought at a profit using platforms like Amazon, Etsy, and eBay.

- Delivery services: Users may make money by delivering items and meals to local clients using services like Amazon Flex, Uber Eats, and DoorDash.

- Pet-sitting and dog-walking: For youngsters who enjoy working with animals and have a flexible schedule, pet sitting and dog walking are excellent ways to get money.

- Babysitting: A dependable and trustworthy babysitter is required by many families to take care of their kids.

The possibilities are limitless, but you must remain dedicated if you want to establish a means of earning.

Types of Income and Taxes

Taxes must typically be paid by teenagers on all income. If you are a teen and you make money through a job or self-employment, you must record that income and pay taxes on it.

Your income level and the tax regulations in your nation will determine how much tax you will have to pay.

In the US, for instance, if a teenager is under the age of 18 and is shown as a dependent on their parent's tax return, their parents will often be liable for paying taxes on their income.

However, if an adolescent is older than 18 or is not shown as a dependent on their parent's tax return, they are in charge of paying taxes on their own income.

It's also important to remember that many nations have a minimum income level below which taxes are not due. This level differs from nation to nation, so it's a good idea to review your nation's tax laws to comprehend the exact rules.

A youngster should be well-versed in taxes and how to file them appropriately so they can make the necessary plans and stay clear of any penalties or fines.

To obtain the most precise data on taxes and income, they might speak with a tax expert or utilize tax software.

Let's look at some different sources of income and the taxes that go along with them:

- Wages and Salaries: This is the most typical source of revenue that workers receive from their occupations. Taxes are normally deducted from every paycheck, and the employee completes a W-4 form to specify how much should be deducted. Additionally, employers are liable for paying a percentage of the employees' taxes.

- Investment Income: This comprises earnings from dividends, interest, and capital gains, among other sources. Taxes must still be paid on investment income even if it is normally taxed at a lower rate than earnings and salaries.

- Self-Employment Income: Self-employed people, such as independent contractors, freelancers, and small business owners, make this kind of money. The employee and employer portions of their income taxes must be paid by self-employed people.

- Rental Income: People who rent out real estate, such a house or an apartment, make this kind of revenue. Individuals may deduct costs associated with the rental property, such as mortgage interest and property taxes, from their taxable income.

- Retirement Income: Retirement funds, like 401(k)s and IRAs, provide this kind of income. Depending on the kind of account, the person's age, and their income level, taxes on retirement income may differ.

- Passive Income: Earnings from investments that need little to no activity, such as stock dividends, real estate rents, and royalties, are used to generate this kind of income. Investment income and passive income are taxed similarly.

Types of Budgeting

You are now legally earning money, thus it is your obligation to understand and learn how to manage your finances. I will show you many techniques of budgeting, and you can then easily put them into practice.

- Envelope Method: The Envelope Method is physically dividing up funds into various envelopes marked for different costs, such as food, entertainment, and savings. If you make $100, for instance, you may set aside $50 for savings, $30 for amusement, and $20 for food. You can only spend as much money as is left in an envelope for a certain category.

- 50/30/20 Rule: According to the 50/30/20 rule, you should budget 50% of your income for essentials, 30% for desires, and 20% for savings and debt reduction. Using $100 as an example, you would set aside $50 for essentials, $30 for desires, and $20 for savings and debt payback.

- Zero-based budgeting: The idea behind zero-based budgeting is to set your income at zero and assign each and every dollar to predetermined spending, savings, and debt reduction. If you have $100, for instance, you may divide it up as follows: $50 for rent and utilities, $20 for transportation, $15 for food, $10 for amusement, and $5 for savings.

- Reverse Budgeting: You establish a budget using reverse budgeting by starting with your savings objectives and working your way backwards. If you had $100, for instance, you may opt to save $50 first, then set aside the other $50 for things like rent, utilities, transportation, groceries, and entertainment.

- Pay Yourself First: With the Pay Yourself First approach, you put saving money ahead of paying bills and other obligations. With a budget of $100, for instance, you would set aside $20 initially, then spend the remaining $80 on things like rent, utilities, transportation, groceries, and entertainment.

- Rolling Budget: With a rolling budget, you set aside money for a predetermined time period, like a month, and then carry any unused cash over to the following one. For instance, if you had $100, you may set aside $50 for rent and utilities, $20 for travel, $15 for groceries, $10 for amusement, and $5 for savings. Any extra cash would be set aside for the budget for the following month.

It is reasonable to argue that you may simply roll it into your investing accounts since some of you will not be responsible for paying rent or other bills as teenagers. Developing these budgeting abilities is also essential since they will enable you to save money in the near future.

How To Create an Investment Plan

Making an investing plan as a teenager might be a terrific approach to start accumulating cash for the future. The following actions can be taken to develop an investing strategy:

- Set financial goals: Decide what you want to accomplish with investing, such as putting money aside for a future education, a vehicle purchase, or an unexpected expense.

- Assess your risk tolerance: Take into account your comfort level with the prospect of losing some or all of your investment. You may use this to decide which investment categories are best for you.

- Create a budget: Choose a monthly investment amount that you can afford to make, and stick to it using any of the techniques I have shown you.

- Research investment options: Look into several investing opportunities that fit your objectives and risk tolerance.

- Diversify your portfolio: You will learn by reading this book to diversify your investments across several asset classes to lower risk.

- Monitor your investments: Make sure you are on pace to attain your goals by monitoring your investments and making modifications as necessary.

- Seek advice: If you require assistance or have any issues, speak with an expert or financial counselor. Remember that investing has a certain amount of risk, and that you should be aware of that risk before you begin investing.

<u>Chapter 3: Diversification is King</u>

John, a buddy of mine, has always had a keen sense of money. He had consistently prospered by making smart investments in mutual funds, equities, bonds, and real estate. As a result, John was keen to invest in 2021 when bitcoin emerged as the hottest new investment possibility.

John transferred all of his holdings out of the conventional markets and invested them all in cryptocurrencies. He had done his homework and was confident that this is the best course of action for him.

He wasn't going to enter the market too late like those other idiots; instead, he was going to enter at the height of the market and profit handsomely.

John's timing was unfortunate since it could not have been worse. When he had invested his whole money, the market started to flip quite swiftly. Before he knew it, his investments had lost 80% of their value.

John was inconsolable. He had lost practically all of his money despite being very certain that this was the proper choice. He had refused to seize the money early when he had the opportunity because he was so engorged with ego and greed. He had practically nothing left at this point.

John had learned a valuable lesson, which stay diversified.

<u>What is Diversification?</u>

Spreading investments across a wide variety of various assets and investments is a key component of the risk management technique known as diversification.

This entails making investments in a range of various equities, bonds, mutual funds, ETFs, commodities, real estate holdings, and other financial instruments.

To minimize the danger of any one investment failing and to increase the possibility of earning returns, diversification is the goal. Investing in equities from many industries or marketplaces, for instance, will reduce an investor's exposure to losses in the event that one of those areas has a downturn.

Similar to this, an investor who holds a combination of bonds, stocks, and other assets—such as real estate or commodities—will be able to gain from the stability of the bonds while still taking part in the potential growth of stocks and alternative investments.

Diversification strategies

There are several tactics to use when investors think of methods to diversify their assets. In order to increase the degree of diversity within a single portfolio, several of the techniques listed below can be combined.

- Asset Allocation: Using this method, you diversify your investments among a variety of assets, including stocks, bonds, mutual funds, and real estate. This lessens the possibility that you will lose everything if one sort of investment fails.

- Sector Investing:This entails making investments across a range of sectors and businesses, including banking, energy, healthcare, and technology. Your portfolio's diversification and risk are lowered as a result.

- International Investing:This tactic entails making investments in businesses located outside of your native nation. This aids in increasing diversity and lowering the risk associated with investing in a single market.

- Value Investing:This entails making investments in inexpensive equities that have the potential to appreciate in value over time. This lowers risk and diversifies your portfolio.

- Growth Investing: This entails making investments in stocks with a high potential for growth. This lowers risk and diversifies your portfolio.

- Hedge Fund Investing: Alternative investments like hedge funds can be utilized to spread out a portfolio's risk and increase diversification. They often carry a larger risk but can result in greater profits.

Pros and Cons of Diversification

Diversification's primary goal is to reduce risk. By spreading your assets over a variety of asset classes, industries, or maturities, you reduce the risk that market shocks will have an identical impact on all of your investments.

Other benefits are also available. Some investors can find investing more fun since diversification allows them to try with a variety of different assets.

Diversification may also increase your chances of finding good news. Positive news affecting several companies rather than just one may be more beneficial to your portfolio.

However, diversification can have certain drawbacks. As a portfolio's holdings grow, it may need more time to manage and may cost more due to the increased transaction fees and brokerage commissions incurred when buying and selling a wider range of assets.

Fundamentally, by spreading out assets, diversification lowers both the risk and the return.

If you invested $100 evenly among six stocks and one of them doubled in value, you would have made a decent profit of $33.32 on your initial $16.66 investment, but not as much as if you had invested all $100 in that one company.

By reducing your possibility for immediate gains, investment diversification protects you from short-term losses. Diverse portfolios typically produce larger long-term benefits.

Pros
- Reduces the risk of the portfolio
- Safeguards against market turbulence
- Offers the possibility of higher long-term returns.
- Investors may find it more enjoyable to research prospective new investments.

Cons

- Limits quick gains
- It requires time to manage.
- Increases the commissions and transaction fees
- It could be confusing for younger, less experienced investors.

<u>What are Over-diversification and Its signs?</u>

Spreading an investing portfolio across an excessive number of various asset classes, industries, and equities is known as over-diversification. Although it is frequently done in an effort to lower risk, it can actually result in underperformance.

Over-diversified investment portfolios show the following symptoms:

- Low returns: An excessively diverse strategy frequently produces worse returns than a portfolio with a narrower emphasis. This is so that prospective profits are not diminished by the expense of purchasing and administering a wide variety of assets.

- Concentration of capital: A portfolio that is too diversified may be unduly focused on a particular industry, asset class, or stock. This may result in more risk and lower rewards.

- High fees: The cost of purchasing and managing each individual investment may pile up over time, making it more expensive to manage a portfolio with an excessive amount of diversification.

- Too much complexity: With more moving components and more choices to be made, a portfolio with an excessive degree of diversification can be challenging to manage. Keeping track of this can be challenging, and mistakes may result.

Chapter 4: Stack the Stock

The origins of stocks and stock markets may be found in medieval Europe, when traders and merchants gathered in marketplaces to trade products and services.

Businesses required a mechanism to raise money when they started to expand and grow so they could pay their operations. The Dutch East India Company started offering stock shares to investors in the 16th century, allowing them to participate in the company's earnings. The current stock market was created at this time.

Philadelphia became the site of the country's first stock exchange in 1790. The New York Stock Exchange (NYSE) didn't come into existence until the 1800s, when the market was tiny and completely uncontrolled. The NYSE immediately rose to prominence and continues to be the top stock exchange in the nation.

In the late 19th and early 20th centuries, the stock market expanded dramatically as major firms rose to prominence as a result of the industrial revolution. As investors flocked to purchase shares in the firms constructing the nation's railroads, the expansion of the railroad sector in particular contributed to the emergence of the stock market.

One of the most infamous and disastrous stock market collapses in history occurred in 1929. The stock market bubble of the 1920s caused stock values to soar, and when the bubble burst, many investors lost their funds. The Great Depression had its start with this occurrence, often known as the Great Crash.

For several years, the stock market was in a slump; it wasn't until the 1950s that things started to turn around. The stock market continued to develop steadily throughout the next decades, reaching new heights by the 1990s.

A fresh wave of investment was stimulated by the development of the internet and online trading, which made it simpler than ever for people to invest in the stock market.

Due to the world financial crisis, the market also fell in 2008 and 2009. The stock market, however, has subsequently bounced back and is expanding.

The stock market nowadays plays a significant role in the expansion and improvement of businesses all over the world and is an essential component of the global economy.

It enables investors to get a return on their investment and firms to raise financing. Additionally, even while it may be unpredictable and dangerous, the stock market can be a potent vehicle for long-term wealth accumulation.

The pace of technological advancement, the status of the global economy, and the regulatory landscape will all have an impact on how the stock market develops in the future.

Future stock trading and management practices might potentially be influenced by the development of fintech and blockchain technologies. Regardless matter what the future holds, the stock market will continue to play a crucial role in the development of the global economy by bringing together investors and businesses.

Quick Facts on Stocks

Are stocks also called shares?

Yes, the terms stocks and shares are frequently used synonymously. Purchasing stock entails acquiring a stake in the firm represented by the stock, which signifies a portion of ownership. When a business issues stock, it is essentially offering ownership shares to the general public, enabling anybody to have a stake in the business. The price of the stock will then fluctuate based on supply and demand once these shares may be purchased and sold on the stock market. As a result, when someone mentions purchasing or selling stocks, they really imply doing it in terms of corporate stock.

Who regulates stock trading?

In the United States, state and federal government organizations oversee stock trading. The Securities and Exchange Commission is the primary body responsible for regulating stock markets and securities trading (SEC). The SEC is an independent federal body tasked with upholding federal securities laws and overseeing the securities sector. Its key goals are to safeguard investors, keep markets fair, orderly, and efficient, and promote capital formation.

The SEC has a number of sections that collaborate to regulate the securities markets, such as the Division of Corporation Finance, which examines periodic reports and registration statements submitted by publicly traded businesses; the Division of Trading and Markets, which regulates trading in securities on stock exchanges, and the Division of Investment Management, which supervises and controls investment firms and investment advisers.

The operations of brokerage companies and investment advisers operating in a state are regulated by state-specific regulatory bodies in addition to the Securities and Exchange Commission (SEC). Investors are meant to be protected by these state organizations, sometimes known as "blue sky" legislation, from fraud and other unethical business activities.

Companies and traders must abide by the stock exchanges' own laws and regulations as well as their own set of self-regulatory requirements.

Self-regulation is implemented by the regulatory division of the exchange, such as the Financial Industry Regulatory Authority (FINRA) and the NYSE Regulation, which collaborates with the SEC and state regulators to regulate trading activity on the exchange.

How to Know a Good Stock

Two popular methods for assessing stocks are fundamental analysis and technical analysis.

Fundamental analysis is a method of examining a firm's financial data and other data to determine the value of the company. The revenue, profitability, debt, and management team of a corporation are some of the factors analysts consider. They assess whether a stock is priced too high or too low in relation to the worth of the firm using this data.

Technical analysis is a technique for analyzing trade data and previous stock prices to forecast future stock price movements. To determine whether a stock is going to rise or fall, this sort of research focuses only on charts and trends.

A company's financial performance and management are evaluated using fundamental analysis, which is like to looking at a report card. Technical analysis is similar to looking at a stock's historical performance to predict how well it will do going forward.

Investors employ one of these methods—or a mix of them—to assess a stock before making a choice. Each has advantages and disadvantages.

A range of perspectives should always be sought before making any conclusions because no approach is failsafe, it's crucial to keep in mind.

Pros of Fundamental analysis

- It offers a thorough grasp of a company's financial situation, which is essential in assessing the long-term prospects of the business and the stock.

- It assists in locating inexpensive equities with the potential for considerable long-term price growth.

- Insights regarding a company's potential for future growth may be gained by examining its management, market trends, and competitors.

- It considers both the qualitative and quantitative components of a firm, giving a more complete picture of the potential of the organization.

Cons of Fundamental analysis

- It might take a lot of time and calls for extensive study and data analysis.

- Due to the possibility of unforeseen occurrences and shifting market conditions, it might not always be correct.

- It may be challenging to determine a company's intrinsic worth, which can cause conflicts among experts.

- It may not be successful in finding short-term trading opportunities since it does not account for short-term market changes.

- For certain businesses, such as those in developing sectors where data and information are few, it might not be effective.

Pros of Technical Analysis

- It's a simple and effective approach to find trends in previous stock price and trading volume data that can predict price changes in the future.

- It is predicated on the notion that patterns seen in previous price movements may be utilized to forecast future price movements and that history has a tendency to repeat itself.

- It may be applied to short-term trading and utilized to find possibilities for short-term trading.

- Finding important levels of support and resistance may be aided by using technical indicators and tools like trend lines and moving averages.

- It may be used to spot overbought or oversold stock circumstances that can portend a market reversal.

Cons of Technical Analysis

- It ignores a company's financial performance or other fundamentals, which might be important in figuring out the long-term prospects of the business and the stock.

- It is predicated on the idea that previous performance serves as an accurate predictor of future performance, which may not always be the case.

- Market manipulation and insider trading may have an impact, which may distort the data and reduce the dependability of trends.

- It may be challenging to decipher charts and patterns, so it's critical to have a solid grasp of technical indicators and tools.

- In turbulent markets with quick and unpredictable price changes, it is not always dependable.

How to Make Money in Stocks

Purchasing and selling stocks with the intention of making a profit requires timing your purchases and sales. Here are some suggestions to help you profit from stocks:

- Research: Spend some time investigating and comprehending the stocks you are interested in. Find out the company's background, financial standing, and future outlook.
- Set Goals: For the equities you purchase, set precise, quantifiable objectives. How much money do you hope to earn? How much time are you prepared to keep the stock?
- Invest wisely: Invest only in stocks you can afford to lose money on. Avoid being sucked into the hype surrounding stocks that appear to be too wonderful to be true.
- Diversify: Diversify the sectors and equities you invest in. Your risk will be lower, and your chances of success will be higher.
- Monitor: Keep an eye on the progress of your investments. Pay attention to market movements and news, and be ready to act swiftly.
- Sell: If the stock isn't performing as you had anticipated, don't be hesitant to sell. Making the most of your sales will help you increase your profitability.

Types of Stocks

Whenever someone thinks of stocks, they often picture shares that are exchanged on stock exchanges. Investors should be aware of the various stock kinds, their characteristics, and potential investment opportunities. To make it simpler for consumers to grasp, we've listed the numerous kinds of stocks that are accessible and divided them into distinct stock classes.

Common & Preferred Stock: Common stock resembles an ownership stake in a business. You acquire a share of the corporation when you purchase common stock. You have more power over the corporation if you possess more common stock.

Preferred stock is a unique kind of stock that has several benefits for you. Regardless of how well the business does, preferred owners receive a set dividend each year. If the firm ever goes out of business, they are also compensated before regular investors.

Common shares may be purchased if you wished to own Google stock. As a result, you would have voting privileges within Google and become a part-owner of the corporation. If you purchased preferred shares, you would get an annual fixed dividend payment before common investors in the event that Google went out of business.

Growth Stocks vs. Value Stocks: There are two distinct stock types: growth stocks and value stocks. Growth stocks are shares of businesses that are anticipated to expand faster than the industry average. They typically trade at greater prices and might be riskier investments. Value stocks are shares of businesses that are trading for less than what they are really worth.

They frequently trade at cheaper prices and might be less hazardous investments. Imagine it like purchasing a new automobile. Growth stocks are similar to purchasing a brand-new sports car in that they are more expensive up front, but you anticipate them to drive quickly and appreciate over time. Value stocks are similar to purchasing a used automobile; they are less expensive, don't come with high expectations for performance, but they may still appreciate in value over time.

Income stocks: Stocks with an income are ones that pay you money! Typically, they are shares of businesses that regularly provide dividends to their shareholders. Companies offer dividends to their shareholders as a way of saying "thank you" for their investments.
Your earnings from income stocks are based on your ownership percentage and the payout rate of the firm. Coca-Cola is a prime example of an income stock.

If you own shares of Coca-Cola, you can receive compensation solely for doing so because the company regularly distributes dividends to its owners.

Blue-Chip Stocks: These are shares of high-quality, well-respected businesses with a lengthy track record of achievement and solid financial performance. Blue-chip stocks include, among others, those of Apple, Microsoft, Coca-Cola, McDonald's, and Johnson & Johnson. Purchasing stock in a reputable firm that is anticipated to be successful for a long time is analogous to investing in blue-chip stocks.

Cyclical and Non-cyclical Stocks: Cyclical equities are ones whose value fluctuates with the state of the economy. They often do better when the economy is robust than when it is poor. Car, furniture, and electronics manufacturers are some examples of cyclical stocks. like Ford, Ikea, and Apple.

Non-cyclical equities have a tendency to be more stable and are less impacted by economic ups and downs. Companies that manufacture goods for the home, medicine, and food are examples of non-cyclical stocks. including Procter & Gamble, Pfizer, and Nestle.

Defensive Stocks: Stocks in firms that generate goods or services that consumers require regardless of the economic or political environment are considered defensive stocks. They are typically regarded as secure investments due to their stable prices and ability to generate consistent revenue. Companies that provide utilities, provide food and beverages, provide healthcare, and manufacture consumer staples are some examples of defensive stocks. such as American Electric Power, PepsiCo, Abbott Laboratories, Duke Energy, Nestle, and Unilever.

IPO Stocks: When a business or other entity decides to offer its shares to the general public and have it traded on the stock market, this is known as an IPO (Initial Public Offering). As an illustration, when Facebook first went public, it made its stocks available to the general public and swiftly rose to the top of the stock market. By doing so, they were able to buy business shares and take advantage of any share price growth.

Penny Stocks: Penny stocks are securities with a share price of under $5. Typically, they are considered high-risk investments since they are shares of obscure, small businesses. Companies in the technology, biotech, and oil and gas sectors are a few examples of penny stocks.

ESG Stocks: ESG stocks are held by businesses that contribute to a better environment, society, and governance. They put an emphasis on issues like lowering their carbon impact, paying their workers fairly, and ensuring that their business methods are moral. Tesla (electric vehicles), Patagonia (sustainable outdoor clothing), and Unilever are some examples of ESG stocks (sustainable food production).

<u>Chapter 5: Bond-Up</u>

Bonds have a long history that extends back to the 1700s. In the early years of the bond market, government-issued bonds were the main source of funding for wars and other significant outlays.

Corporate bonds were created in the 1800s and issued by businesses to obtain money for operations and projects. Early in the 20th century, financial organizations started issuing bonds as a strategy to diversify their holdings, making bonds more broadly accessible to investors.

The creation of the New York Stock Exchange Bond Market in the 1920s marked the start of the modern age of bond trading. Individual investors may now purchase and sell bonds in a more structured and regulated environment thanks to the NYSE Bond Market.

The establishment of the secondary market for bonds in the 1950s prompted continued expansion of the bond market. This made trading bonds for investors simpler and more effective by enabling them to purchase and sell bonds directly from and to the issuer.

A genuinely global bond market was established in the 1960s with the advent of the Eurobond market, which allowed investors to purchase and sell bonds in any currency.

Bond market growth continued throughout the 1970s as a result of the expansion of the global bond market. This made it possible for investors to purchase and sell bonds across national borders, establishing a genuinely global bond market.

The growth of the junk bond market in the 1980s gave investors the chance to participate in bonds with high risks and potential returns.

Due to their ability to produce a consistent source of income, their relative safety, and the fact that they are quite liquid, bonds continue to be a popular investment choice for investors today. The bond market has expanded considerably in recent years and is now a substantial component of the global financial system.

What are Bonds?

Bonds are simply loans you may provide to a business, the government, or another institution. When you purchase a bond, you are effectively lending the issuer money, which they agree to repay you with interest at a later period. Regularly, often once a year or every six months, the issuer will pay you interest. The bond's issuer reimburses you for the initial sum you lent them when the bond expires. In essence, you are lending money when you purchase a bond and receiving interest in return.

Types of Bonds

Government Bonds: Governments typically issue government bonds to finance public projects or to pay for administrative costs. Due to their government backing and relatively lower interest rates than other bonds, these bonds are widely regarded as being extremely secure investments.

Corporate Bonds: Businesses issue corporate bonds to generate money for a variety of tasks or to fund operations. They sometimes have higher interest rates than government bonds, but they also come with a greater risk because the corporation issuing the bond could stop making payments.

Municipal Bonds: Local governments typically issue municipal bonds to raise money for public projects. Since they are guaranteed by the government, they are typically regarded as secure investments and provide tax-free interest income.

Zero Coupon Bonds: Bonds with zero coupon rates are repaid for their entire face value at maturity rather than making regular interest payments. These bonds are frequently utilized as long-term investments because of their minimal risk.

Convertible Bonds: Bonds that are convertible at a specified price into shares of the issuer's equity are known as convertible bonds. Since the value of the underlying shares might decline, these bonds provide larger rewards but also more risk.

High-Yield Bonds: High-yield bonds come with greater interest rates than other bond kinds, but they also come with more risk because they are typically issued by businesses with poorer credit ratings. Usually, these bonds are bought for speculation.

Bond Pricing

The price paid for a bond is referred to as its pricing. It depends on the bond's interest rate, how long it has until it matures, and market interest rates at the time. Bond pricing is just like buying a vehicle. The price of the automobile will increase in direct proportion to its features and condition. Bonds work in a similar manner. The bond will cost more the longer its period and the higher its interest rate. Bonds with shorter periods and lower interest rates will be less expensive.

Bond Ratings

Bond ratings provide insight into a bond's likelihood of repaying its investors. They can be rated anywhere between AAA (the highest) to D and are determined by rating organizations like Moody's and Standard & Poor's (the lowest). Bonds with a AAA rating are considered to be the safest investments since they have a significantly better likelihood of repaying investors than bonds with a lower grade. Additionally, compared to other investment options, AAA bonds are thought to be less risky. Bonds with lower ratings are significantly riskier since they are less likely to repay investors and may potentially lose all of their value. Therefore, before investing in a bond, it's crucial to grasp its rating.

Bond Yields

Bond yields are the sum of money that a bond will eventually pay out. When you buy a bond, you are effectively lending money to the issuer—typically a government or business—for a certain period of time. Bonds are stated as percentages. The yield is derived by factoring in the interest rate, the duration you will keep the bond for, and the price you paid for it. It represents the amount of money you will get from the bond in exchange for your loan. As an illustration, if you purchase a bond with a 10% interest rate and keep it for five years, you will earn 10% of the bond's initial purchase price per year for the next five years.

Bond Investing Strategies

Research the Basics of Bond Investing: It's crucial to comprehend the many sorts of bonds accessible and how they function before making an investment in them. Making educated selections may be aided by reading up on the fundamentals of bond investing, such as what bonds are, the many kinds of bonds, and bond pricing.

Consider Investing in Low-Risk Bonds: Government bonds and other low-risk bonds are typically thought of as safer investments than other forms of bonds. Low-risk bond investments can assist lower your risk of financial loss and can offer a reliable source of income.

Build a Bond Ladder: Bond laddering is a financial investment technique that involves buying several bonds with various maturities, such as one-, five-, and ten-year bonds. This tactic can aid in reducing volatility and spreading out your risk.

Choose Shorter term Bonds: Since they are less likely to face price changes as a result of shifting interest rates, shorter-term bonds are often less hazardous than longer-term bonds. Shorter-term bonds can assist to lower your chance of financial loss.

Stay Diversified: Even when investing in bonds, it's still vital to diversify your portfolio. Your risk of losing money can be decreased by investing in a variety of bonds, including corporate, governmental, and municipal bonds.

Invest with a Roth IRA: A Roth IRA is an investment vehicle created for long-term tax-advantaged investments. Bond investments made through a Roth IRA can lower your tax bill and help you save for retirement.

Utilize a Financial advisor: Making the greatest choices for your investing objectives may be ensured by using a financial advisor's services. You may build a portfolio that is customized to your needs with the assistance of a financial advisor by selecting the appropriate bonds.

Compare Bond Fund Fees: Fees including management fees and sales charges are frequently attached to bond funds. Before making an investment, it is crucial to examine the costs of several bond funds to ensure you are receiving the best deal.

Start Small and Increase Gradually: Bond investing might involve a lengthy commitment, so it's crucial to start modest and build up gradually. Reduced risk can be achieved by starting small and growing your investments over time.

Bond Market Risks

Interest Rate Risk: The danger of rising interest rates depreciating the value of current bonds is known as interest rate risk. Bond prices normally decline when rates rise, so this may happen when they do.

Credit Risk: Credit risk is the possibility that the bond's issuer won't be able to make principle and interest payments. This could happen if the issuer's finances worsen to the point that they can no longer pay their debts.

Inflation Risk: The risk of inflation is the possibility that higher prices may make the bond's payments less valuable. This might happen when fixed payments lose some of their real value due to rising inflation.

Reinvestment Risk: Reinvestment risk is the chance that coupon payments will not grow at the same rate as the initial bond if they are reinvested. This might happen if interest rates decline and the payments are reinvested at a rate that is lower than the bond's initial yield.

Liquidity Risk: The danger that a bond won't be able to be sold promptly or for its full value is known as liquidity risk. This may happen if there aren't many buyers available.

Bond Swaps

In a bond swap, an investor trades a bond they already possess for another bond of a different type or with different conditions. A bond with a fixed interest rate could be swapped out for one with an adjustable interest rate, for instance, by an investor. In order to achieve their financial objectives, the investor effectively exchanges one bond for another. You're making a transaction with the intention of expanding your wardrobe, much as when you swap out a pair of pants for a new pair.

Chapter 6: Ring REITs

Real estate investment trusts, or REITs, are financial instruments that let investors purchase a variety of assets with a real estate component.

When Congress enacted the Cigar Excise Tax Extension in 1960, they made their debut in the United States. The development of publicly listed REITs that would be free from federal income taxes was made possible by this act.

REITs have gained popularity since they were first established. With a market value of around $1.2 trillion as of 2021, there are more than 200 publicly listed REITs.

REITs are often set up as closed-end funds, which means that the fund management owns every investment while allowing investors to buy shares of the fund. Investors are eligible for dividends and capital gains when the fund performs successfully since these shares represent a component of the fund.

Diversification, liquidity, and access to experienced management are just a few advantages that REITs may provide to investors. Additionally, they give investors the chance to invest in real estate-related assets without having to buy or manage actual real estate.

Both individual investors and institutional investors, including pension funds and life insurance organizations, like REITs as an investment.

Despite being a relatively new investment instrument, REITs have been operating for more than 60 years. Because of this, they frequently come with substantial risks and are vulnerable to significant market volatility. However, investors might benefit from investing in REITs if they have a well-diversified portfolio and conduct thorough research.

Benefits of Investing in REITs

Diversification: Investors' total risk can be decreased by investing in REITs, which can offer a diverse portfolio of income-producing real estate assets.

Liquidity: Investors can access the real estate industry by purchasing REITs rather than actual buildings. Due to the ability to purchase and sell REIT shares on the stock market, investors have access to liquidity and can quickly exit their investment.

Professional Management: In order to profit from the experience of seasoned experts without having to manage the properties themselves, REITs use professional management teams to oversee real estate assets.

Passive Income: Investors who own REITs get payments on a monthly or quarterly basis as a reliable source of income. Investors get a consistent stream of passive income from these payouts, which are normally taxed as regular income.

Affordable Entry Points: Investors may find it more economical to enter the real estate industry by making an investment in REITs. When compared to purchasing real estate, REITs often demand significantly lower initial investments, making them a desirable choice for those with limited funds.

Factors to Consider Before Investing in REITs

Risk Appetite: Before making an investment in REITs, investors should think about their risk tolerance. REITs may be risky investments, therefore not all investors may want to consider them.

Investment Goals: Before purchasing REITs, investors should think about their investment objectives. Although REITs are frequently used to provide income, they can also be utilized to increase capital.

Fees and Expenses: Investors should think about the costs and fees related to buying REITs. Management fees, running expenditures, and other costs are a few examples of these charges.

Market Conditions: Before making an investment in REITs, investors should take the current market circumstances into account. The health of the economy and the real estate industry as a whole can have an influence on REITs.

Management Team: Investors should think about the REIT's management team before making an investment. A capable and knowledgeable management team may aid in maximizing profits and lowering risk.

Types of REITs

Retail REITs: About 24% of REIT investments are made in shopping centers and independent retail. This is the biggest investment of its sort ever undertaken in the country of America.

Any shopping center you often frequent is probably owned by a REIT. Before even considering investing in retail real estate, it is essential to do a comprehensive analysis of the retail industry. What does the future look like? Is it now financially sound?

Remember that the way that retail REITs make money is through charging tenants rent. It's possible for merchants who are experiencing cash flow problems as a result of slow sales to delay or even skip payments, which would ultimately drive them into bankruptcy.

After you've assessed the industry, you should focus your attention on the REITs themselves. They must produce healthy earnings, keep strong balance sheets, and carry as little debt as possible, just like with any investment (especially the short-term kind).

Retail REITs with sizable cash reserves will have the opportunity to buy desirable properties at a discount during an economic downturn. The businesses that are run most effectively will use this.

However, as more and more people choose to shop online rather than in conventional malls, there are longer-term concerns for the retail REIT sector. Despite the pressure on the sub-sector, landlords have kept coming up with new ways to fill their properties with offices and other non-retail-focused tenants.

Residential REITs: Both prefabricated houses and multifamily rental apartment buildings are owned and managed by these REITs. One should consider a number of factors before to purchasing this type of REIT.

For instance, the best apartment markets often reside in regions with relatively high housing costs relative to the rest of the country.

More people are obliged to rent as a result of the high cost of single-family homes in areas like New York and Los Angeles, which drives up the monthly rent that landlords may charge. As a result, the largest residential REITs usually focus on important urban centers.

Investors should keep an eye on a market's population and employment growth. When there is a net inflow of people to an area, the economy is usually growing and employment is simple to find. A decreasing vacancy rate and rising rents indicate that demand has improved.

As long as there is a constrained supply of flats in a certain market and the demand is growing, residential REITs should perform well. The firms with the strongest balance sheets and greatest capital tend to do the best, just like with all enterprises.

Healthcare REITs: Healthcare REITs will be a fascinating sub-sector to watch as Americans become older and healthcare costs grow. Healthcare REITs invest in a variety of assets, including hospitals, clinics, nursing homes, and retirement communities.

The health care system has a direct impact on the performance of this real estate. The majority of the proprietors of these facilities rely on private donations, Medicare and Medicaid reimbursements, and occupancy fees. As long as healthcare funding is a mystery, so are healthcare REITs.

You should search for two characteristics in a healthcare REIT: investments in a variety of property types and a varied customer base.

FAQ (frequently asked questions) on REITS

Are REITs Good Investment?

REIT investments are a great method to diversify your portfolio beyond conventional equities and bonds because of their strong dividend yields and potential for long-term capital development.

What REITs Should I Invest In?

The risks and possible benefits associated with each type of REIT vary depending on the state of the economy. Through a REIT ETF, investors may invest in the REIT market without directly dealing with the sector's complexities.

How do you Make Money on REITs?

Since REITs are required by the IRS to distribute 90% of their taxable income to shareholders, REIT dividends are usually significantly higher than the ordinary stock on the S&P 500. One of the best ways to benefit from the passive income of REITs is to compound these high-yield dividends.

Can You Lose Money on REITs?

Any investment has the risk of losing money. Publicly traded REITs are more susceptible to a fall in value when interest rates rise and more capital is frequently placed in bonds as a result.

How To Invest in REITs

Teenagers typically purchase REITs through their custodian or parent's brokerage account.

When it comes to managing and safeguarding a minor's assets until they reach the age of majority, a custodian is often a parent or guardian (18 or 21). A teenager may be allowed to form a separate custodial brokerage account or buy REITs straight from the custodian's account, depending on the sort of account the custodian has.

An alternative is for a young person to think about investing in REITs through a mutual fund or exchange-traded fund (ETF). In order to lower the risk associated with investing in a single REIT, mutual funds and ETFs can offer diversified exposure to the REIT market.

Additionally, compared to individual REITs, mutual funds and ETFs are frequently more affordable and liquid, making them appropriate for younger investors.

And last, a kid could be able to buy REITs through an internet investment site. Numerous REITs are available on most internet platforms, and many of them also include instructional materials to assist novice investors in making wise choices.

Although, to some extent, distributing your risk is preferable than focusing.

In general, the industry of healthcare real estate benefits from the increase in demand for healthcare services (which should occur with an older population).

As a consequence, in addition to a diversity of customers and property types, look for companies that have a deep understanding of the healthcare industry, strong financial standings, and enough access to affordable financing.

Office REITs: Investments in office buildings are made by office REITs. They receive rental income from their tenants who are tied by long-term leases. There are four issues that everyone thinking about investing in an office REIT has to address.

-What are the unemployment rate and the state of the economy?
-What are the vacancy rates like?
-How is the local economy doing where the REIT invests?
-What amount of funds is available for purchases?

Look for REITs that invest in booming industries. It is preferable to own a bunch of unremarkable structures in Washington, D.C. as opposed to, example, having fantastic office space in Detroit.

Mortgage REITs: Mortgages represent around 10% of the assets of a REIT, compared to real estate. The most well-known options—though not usually the best—are Fannie Mae and Freddie Mac. As firms supported by the government, they buy mortgages on the secondary market.

Risks still exist even if this particular type of REIT invests in mortgages rather than stocks. The book value of mortgage REITs would decrease as a result of higher interest rates, which would lead to lower stock prices.

A large portion of the capital of mortgage REITs will also come from secured and unsecured loan offerings. A loan portfolio's value will decrease when interest rates rise since further funding will cost more.

In a low-interest-rate environment with a chance of rising rates, the majority of mortgage REITs trade below their net asset value (nAV) per share. It's challenging to find the perfect one.

Are REITs Safe During Recession?

Some types of REITs, like those that control hotel properties, are not the ideal investments during an economic slump. Purchasing a variety of real estate, such as a hospital or retail space, is a great way to hedge against a recession. They are less cyclical as a result of their longer lease agreements.

Chapter 7: Let's Get Mutual

The existence of mutual funds dates back to the late 19th century. The first mutual fund was established in the Netherlands in 1822 to assist investors in reducing risk and diversifying their assets.

Since then, mutual funds have grown in popularity as a means of investing since they provide investors access to a range of asset classes and industries while enabling them to diversify their portfolios without having to buy individual stocks and bonds.

Banks and insurance firms first developed mutual funds as a method to aggregate money from many participants and provide a wider selection of assets than an individual investor could.

Mutual funds, which combine the money of many participants, can give access to a variety of investments, including stocks, bonds, and other asset classes including real estate and commodities.

Massachusetts Investors Trust established the first mutual fund in the US in 1924. With the help of this fund, investors were able to diversify their holdings over a range of stocks, bonds, and other assets.

Mutual funds have gained popularity since then and are currently among the most widely used investment vehicles for both retail and institutional investors.

Banks, investment consultants, and brokerages are just a few of the financial organizations that currently provide mutual funds.

They can also be found on internet platforms like robo-advisors and ETFs. A lot of 401(k) and IRA plans include access to a selection of mutual funds, making them a popular choice for retirement savings.

What are Mutual Funds?

An investment vehicle known as a mutual fund pools the money of its shareholders to buy securities including stocks, bonds, money market instruments, and other assets.

Mutual funds are managed by qualified money managers who distribute the assets with the goal of boosting investors' income or capital gains. The construction and maintenance of a mutual fund's portfolio reflect the investment goals stated in the prospectus.

Mutual funds give novice or individual investors access to portfolios of stocks, bonds, and other assets that are expertly managed.

Each shareholder therefore shares proportionately in the fund's gains or losses.

Mutual funds invest in a wide range of assets, and their performance is frequently gauged by the change in the market value of the fund as a whole, which is generated from the performance of all of their underlying investments put together.

The bulk of mutual funds are housed by large financial institutions like Fidelity Investments, Vanguard, T. Rowe Price, and Oppenheimer.

A mutual fund has a fund manager, sometimes referred to as its investment adviser, who is legally required to operate in the shareholders' best interests.

Types of Mutual Funds

Although there are several types of mutual funds available for purchase, the bulk of them may be divided into the following four basic categories: stock funds, money market funds, bond funds, and target-date funds.

Stock Funds: As its name implies, this fund primarily invests in stocks or equities. This category includes a number of subcategories. Depending on the size of the companies they invest in, equity funds are referred to as small-, mid-, or large-cap. Others can be distinguished by the way they invest, such as those that focus on aggressive growth, income, value, and other factors. Another approach to categorize equity funds is based on whether they invest in local (U.S.) stocks or foreign equities.

Bond Funds: Mutual funds known as "Bond Funds" invest in bonds, including corporate, governmental, and municipal bonds. These funds are riskier than money market funds yet have better returns. Because there are so many different types of bonds, bond funds can vary greatly depending on where they invest, and all bond funds are susceptible to interest rate risk.

Index Funds: Index funds invest in stocks that mirror key market indices, such as the S&P 500 or the Dow Jones Industrial Average (DJIA). Because this strategy necessitates less research from analysts and advisors and resulting in cheaper expenses being passed on to shareholders, these funds are usually developed with cost-conscious investors in mind.

Balanced Funds: Balanced funds incorporate a variety of asset classes such as stocks, bonds, money market instruments, alternative investments, and others. The objective of this fund, sometimes referred to as an asset allocation fund, is to lower exposure risk across asset classes.

Some funds' definitions contain a fixed allocation method, giving investors a predictable exposure to various asset classes. For the purpose of achieving various investor objectives, some funds use a dynamic allocation percentages method. This may entail adjusting to changing market circumstances, personal life transitions, or changes in the business cycle.

When necessary to maintain the integrity of the fund's stated strategy, the portfolio manager is usually granted the freedom to alter the asset class ratio.

Income Funds: To regularly provide current income is the objective of income funds, after which they are called. These funds invest primarily in reputable corporate and government bonds, holding them until maturity to generate interest income. The major objective of these funds is to provide investors with steady cash flow, despite the possibility that fund assets can appreciate in value. Therefore, the target market for these products consists of retirees and cautious investors.

International/Global Funds: An international fund, sometimes referred to as a foreign fund, only invests in assets that are located elsewhere. Global funds, on the other hand, have the flexibility to invest anywhere in the world. The nation's unique political and economic risks typically have an impact on their volatility. However, because outcomes in other countries could not be related to returns in the country of origin, these funds can be added to a well-balanced portfolio by adding variety.

Specialty Funds: Specialty mutual funds are those that focus on a certain market or sector. By taking on more risks and investing in a specific asset class, such as energy, technology, or healthcare, these funds seek to outperform regular funds.

The majority of the time, specialized funds are managed by seasoned personnel with a focus on market research and industry analysis. These funds are riskier than conventional funds and may need bigger minimum commitments. These funds may give higher returns if the sector or industry outperforms the broader market, but there is also a potential that they might experience a loss.

How to Invest in a Mutual Funds

Mutual funds may be purchased using a custodial account opened in a minor's name and controlled by a guardian. This guardian has the power to manage the account until the child reaches legal age, often 18 or 21, in which case other adults are responsible. Custodial account laws tend to be uniform among states, despite the possibility that they might differ greatly.

The Uniform Gifts to Minors Act (UGMA) or the Uniform Transfer to Minors Act (UTMA), which specify the guidelines for handling and administering a minor's account, are frequently followed while creating accounts. Most states provide UTMA accounts, which can help reduce taxes. In UTMA mutual fund accounts, gains up to $1,100 are tax-free; profits beyond that amount are subject to the minor's tax rate. The parent's rate of taxes is applied to earnings beyond $2,200 per year.

Pros of Mutual Fund Investing

Professional Management: Professional money managers who are equipped with the necessary resources, expertise, and understanding oversee the management of mutual funds. This may lower the likelihood of losses occurring while increasing profits.

Low Minimum Investments: It is possible to purchase mutual funds for a relatively small minimum investment. As a result, many different types of investors can access them.

Liquidity: Mutual funds are easily convertible into cash and are liquid investments. They are thus a practical choice for investors that want immediate access to their funds.

Cons of Mutual Fund Investing

Fees & Expenses: The costs and fees associated with mutual funds can lower total results.

Lack of Control: Investors have little influence over just how their funds are invested while using mutual funds, which are handled by seasoned money managers.

Risk: Investors who invest in mutual funds run the risk of not getting their original investment returned.

Tax Implication: Taxes on capital gains may apply when assets in mutual funds are sold.

Chapter 8: Play ETFs

Since the early 1990s, exchange-traded funds (ETFs) have existed. In 1993, Standard & Poor's Depositary Receipts (SPDRs), the first ETF, was launched. The S&P 500 index was intended to be tracked by SPDRs, and each share of an ETF represented a portion of the index.

Since then, ETFs have grown in popularity, with a wide range of ETF kinds offering a range of investing strategies and covering a wide range of markets. These days, ETFs may be found on a wide range of markets, including those for commodities, currencies, and securities like stocks and bonds.

ETFs started to provide more actively managed products in the early 2000s. This removed the requirement for a conventional mutual fund and allowed investors to participate directly in a certain strategy or asset class.

This made it possible for investors to use a single investment to access a range of asset classes and strategies.

As investors search for strategies to diversify their portfolios without having to handle a huge number of individual equities and bonds, ETFs are growing in popularity today.

ETFs give investors the option to trade more rapidly and inexpensively than conventional mutual funds.

ETFs have developed into a crucial tool for investors looking to diversify their portfolios while utilizing the affordable trading fees and ease of use offered by exchanges. For investors seeking to access many markets, strategies, and asset classes with a single investment, ETFs are a compelling choice.

What is an ETF?

A type of pooled financial asset that performs very similarly to mutual funds is exchange-traded funds (ETFs). Exchange-traded funds (ETFs) can be purchased or sold on a stock market similarly to traditional equities, in contrast to mutual funds, which are solely accessible to institutional investors.

ETFs frequently track a certain index, industry, commodity, or other asset. An ETF may be created to track anything, from the price of a single commodity to a vast and diverse group of assets. Even ETFs may be created to adhere to specific investing strategies.

Understanding ETF?

Exchange-traded funds (ETFs) are so-called because they trade on exchanges like stocks do. As shares are bought and sold on the market during the trading day, an ETF's share price will change.

Mutual funds, on the other hand, cannot transact more than once per day and are not traded on an exchange. ETFs are usually less expensive and more liquid than mutual funds.

ETFs contain a range of underlying assets as opposed to stocks, which only hold one underlying asset. Because they hold a range of assets, ETFs are widely utilized for diversification.

As a result, several types of assets, such as stocks, commodities, bonds, or a mix of investments, can be found in ETFs.

A single sector or industry may be the only thing that an ETF invests in, or it may hold hundreds or thousands of stocks from many industries. Others have a global orientation, while some funds focus only on U.S. offers.

In banking-focused ETFs, for instance, stocks of various banks from throughout the sector may be present.

Because an ETF is a marketable investment, it can be sold for a loss and has a share price that makes it easy to purchase and sell it on exchanges at any time of the day. As open-ended funds by design, the majority of US ETFs are subject to the Investment Company Act of 1940 until further rules modify this.

Types of ETFs

A number of ETFs are available to investors, who may use them to produce income, control risk in their portfolios, engage in speculation and price appreciation, and manage risk. Here is a brief rundown of some of the ETFs that are available right now.

Passive and Active ETFs: Passive ETFs are defined as investments that track a certain market index, such as the S&P 500. Since the goal of these funds is to closely resemble the performance of the index, active management is not required to choose which investments to buy or sell.

A useful comparison for adolescents is that a passive ETF is like a robot that repeats the same set of instructions. A passive ETF is the SPDR S&P 500 ETF, for instance (SPY).

Active ETFs, on the other hand, are funds that are actively managed by a licensed money manager. This shows that the manager, rather than just keeping an eye on an index, is looking for assets that will exceed the market.

An active ETF may be likened to a race car driver who is looking for the best track to win the race, driven by a teenager. An active ETF would be one like the iShares Core S&P 500 ETF (IVV).

Bond ETFs: Bond ETFs allow for regular income for investors. The distribution of their income is influenced by how well the underlying bonds perform. They might be corporate, municipal, state and local, or government bonds. Unlike the underlying assets they hold, bond ETFs don't have a maturity date. They typically trade above or below the price of the actual bond.

Stock ETFs: Stock (equity) ETFs are made up of a group of stocks that follow a certain sector or industry. For example, a stock ETF may track stocks in the international or car industries. Giving a single industry with both established players and up-and-coming competitors with development potential a variety of exposure is the aim.

Industry/Sector ETFs: ETFs that focus on certain industries or sectors are known as sectors or industries. For instance, companies working in the energy industry will be included in an ETF for that sector. By tracking the performance of the companies that make up a sector, industry ETFs are intended to give investors exposure to that industry's prospective development.

One such is the recent financial infusion into the IT sector. Since ETFs do not need direct ownership of shares, the negative consequences of variable stock performance are also constrained. Industry ETFs are widely used to migrate between sectors throughout economic cycles.

Commodity ETFs: As their name implies, commodity ETFs invest in commodities like gold or crude oil. Commodity ETFs have a variety of benefits. A portfolio is initially diversified, which makes it easier to manage downturns.

For example, commodity ETFs can act as a cushion during a decline in the stock market. Second, purchasing a commodity outright is more expensive than investing in a commodities ETF. In order for the former to avoid having to pay for storage and insurance.

Currency ETFs: Through currency exchange-traded funds, the performance of currency pairings that combine local and foreign currencies is monitored (ETFs). The uses of ETFs that invest in currencies are numerous.

They may be used to forecast currency prices depending on the political and economic tendencies of a country. They are also used by exporters and importers as a hedge against volatile overseas markets or to diversify their portfolios. Some of them are also used as hedges against inflation. There is even an ETF for bitcoin.

Inverse ETFs: Inverse ETFs strive to profit from market declines by shorting stocks. Selling a stock in expectation of its value falling and then buying it again at a loss is known as shorting. An inverse ETF uses derivatives to short a stock. They are essentially bets against the market.

When the market declines, an inverse ETF gains value accordingly. Investors should be aware that a large number of inverse exchange-traded funds (ETFs) are exchange-traded notes (ETNs) rather than legitimate ETFs. An ETN is a bond even though it trades like a stock and has a bank as its issuer. Check with your broker to see whether an ETN might be an appropriate addition to your portfolio.

Leveraged ETFs: Leveraged ETFs are a subclass of ETFs (Exchange Traded Funds) that use financial instruments like derivatives to increase the possible profits on an investment. This suggests that while Leveraged ETFs offer a bigger potential for profit than Regular ETFs, they also have a higher potential for risk.

Think about it: if you held a common ETF that followed the stock market and it grew by 1% in a single day, your investment would have grown by 1%. However, you may have profited 2% or more on that same day if you bought a leveraged ETF. However, if the stock market dropped by 1%, a Leveraged ETF would cause you to lose 2% or more.

You may therefore maximize your gains by using leveraged ETFs, but there is also a bigger risk involved.

Here is an illustration. Take into account investing in a leveraged exchange-traded fund (ETF) that tracks the S&P 500. On a good day, your investment could return 3%, but on a bad day, it might return 6%. Therefore, if you're willing to take on additional risk, leveraged ETFs might help you increase your financial gains, but they could also increase your losses.

What to Look for in an ETFs

Before buying any ETFs, investors must first fund their brokerage account. The specific techniques for financing your brokerage account will be determined by your broker.

After opening an account, you may browse for ETFs and make purchases and sells exactly like you would with ordinary shares. One of the best ways to narrow down your choice of ETFs is to use an ETF screening tool.

Several brokers offer these tools to help customers navigate the many different ETF products. ETFs may frequently be located by applying some of the criteria listed below:

Commissions: Many ETFs have commission-free trading, which means there are no fees for placing the transaction. Even so, it's critical to assess if this may be a deal-breaker.

Holdings: The portfolios of other funds are commonly taken into consideration by screener systems, allowing consumers to compare the various holdings of each possible ETF buy.

Performance: This is a standard metric used to compare ETFs, despite the fact that past performance does not predict future outcomes.

Expenses: The expense ratio will be lower as less of your funds are used for administrative costs. Despite the temptation to always seek for funds with the lowest cost ratios, occasionally more expensive funds (such as actively managed ETFs) have strong enough performance to more than justify the higher fees.

Volume: The trading volume of various funds may be used to gauge how popular they were over a certain time period; the higher the volume, the easier it may be to trade that fund.

<u>Common Examples of ETFs</u>

Here are a few current examples of well-known ETFs. While some ETFs specialize on certain sectors, others follow stock indices to create wider portfolios.

- Exchange-traded funds (ETFs) for commodities provide representation of markets for commodities including gold (GLD), silver (SLV), crude oil (USO), and natural gas (UNG).
- Sector ETFs cover a variety of specific industries and sectors, including oil (OIH), energy (XLE), financial services (XLF), real estate investment trusts (IYR), and biotechnology (BBH).

- The Dow Jones Industrial Average's 30 stocks are represented by the SPDR Dow Jones Industrial Average (DIA) ("diamonds").
- A common component of the Nasdaq 100 Index, which is monitored by the Invesco QQQ (QQQ), includes technology companies ("cubes").
- The iShares Russell 2000 small-cap index is the next index (IWM).
- The most well-known and oldest S&P 500 index-tracking ETF still in existence is SPY, the SPDR S&P 500 ETF.
- Although they are traded in the US and are priced in USD, country ETFs track the major stock indexes of other countries. Israel, Brazil, China (MCHI), Japan (EWJ), and China (EWZ) are a few instances (EIS). Some individuals follow developed market economies (DMEs) while others follow emerging market economies (EMEs) (EFA).

How to Invest and Buy an ETFs

Research ETFs: It's crucial for teenagers to comprehend the fundamentals of ETF investing. Find more about the various ETF kinds, their costs, and the advantages and hazards of investing in them.

Open an Investment Account: You must create a brokerage account before you can invest in ETFs. If you're a teen, you might need a parent or other adult to assist you with opening the account. Open a Roth IRA account if you want to save and invest for retirement without having to pay taxes on any of your income.

Set Financial Goals: Prior to investing in ETFs, it's critical to have a financial strategy and be aware of your objectives. Think about your short- and long-term objectives as well as your risk tolerance.

Start Investing: You may begin investing once you have a financial strategy in place and are familiar with the ETFs you wish to use. Be sure to diversify your holdings and keep in mind the ETF fees that may apply.

Monitor & Rebalance: It's crucial to keep an eye on your assets as you construct your portfolio and rebalance it as necessary. Rebalancing aids in ensuring that you preserve a diverse portfolio and manage your risk.

Pros of ETFs

1. Reduced Cost ETFs are more cost-effective investments than mutual funds due to their lower fee ratios.

2. Greater Trading Flexibility: Unlike mutual funds, which are only priced once at the end of the trading day, ETFs can be exchanged at any time throughout the trading day.

3. Tax Efficiency: Because ETFs produce smaller capital gains than mutual funds, they are more tax efficient than the latter.

4. Diversification: Using ETFs allows investors to obtain exposure to a variety of assets without having to buy each one separately.

Cons of ETFs

1. Higher Transaction Costs: Compared to traditional investing, ETFs could come with a higher transaction cost.

2. Tracking Inaccuracies: It's possible that ETFs don't correctly reflect the performance of the underlying index or benchmark.

3. Lack of Liquidity: ETFs may not be as liquid as traditional assets, which can result in large bid-ask spreads.

4. Risk associated with leverage: Because leveraged ETFs employ loans and derivatives to increase profits, they might be hazardous investments.

Chapter 9: Commodity Zone

Since the dawn of human civilization, tribes and newly established kingdoms have exchanged products for food, resources, and other items through bartering and trading.

In actuality, commodity trade predates stock and bond trading by many centuries.

Ancient Greece and Rome were able to establish complex commercial networks and permit the exchange of products across vast territories thanks to trade routes like the well-known Silk Road, which linked Europe and the Far East. This ability is directly tied to the rise of these empires.

In the present era, commodities are still traded widely around the globe. The development of derivatives markets and exchanges has also increased complexity. By regulating and standardizing the trading of commodities, exchanges create markets that are effective and liquid.

The largest contemporary commodities market is probably the Chicago Board of Trade (CBOT), which was established in 1848. To help producers and consumers of commodities manage risk by minimizing price uncertainty, it first limited its trading to agricultural commodities including wheat, corn, and soybeans.

It now provides options and futures contracts on a wide range of products, including energy, gold, silver, U.S. Treasury bonds, and many more.

Following the merger of the Chicago Board of Trade (CBOT) and the Chicago Mercantile Exchange (CME) Group in 2007, the group's agricultural product offerings were expanded to include interest rates and stock index items.

A few commodities exchanges have merged or shut down in recent years. Even while some exchanges concentrate on a certain category, the majority of them only carry a few unique commodities.

In the middle of the 2000s, the Chicago Mercantile Exchange (CME) in the US acquired three more commodities exchanges. CME originally acquired the Chicago Board of Trade (CBOT) in 2007 before purchasing the New York Mercantile Exchange (NYMEX) and the Commodity Exchange, Inc. in 2008. (COMEX).

The four markets make up the CME Group. After the merger of the New York Board of Trade and Intercontinental Exchange (ICE), ICE Futures U.S. was established in 2007. Each exchange offers a variety of global benchmarks for the most significant asset classes.

What is Commodity Markets

A commodities market is where different items are bought and sold. Similar to a grocery store, however here people purchase non-food items like wheat, gold, or oil. Prices for these commodities may increase or decrease based on their availability and how much consumers are willing to spend.

Commodities are frequently separated into two groups: hard commodities and soft commodities. Hard commodities are raw materials that need to be mined or exploited, as opposed to soft commodities, which are agricultural products or animals such as maize, wheat, coffee, sugar, soybeans, and pigs. Gold, rubber, and oil are a few examples of hard commodities.

How Commodities Market Work

Producers and consumers can purchase commodities on controlled, liquid marketplaces provided by commodity exchanges.

These market participants can also make use of commodities derivatives to guarantee future demand or output. In addition, investors, arbitrageurs, and speculators are active players in these markets.

Diversifying a portfolio with a variety of commodities as an alternative asset class can help, and some commodities, like precious metals, have historically been thought of as the best inflation hedges.

Due to the fact that commodity prices typically move in opposition to stock values, some investors also resort to them during times of market instability.

In the past, trading in commodities was mostly the purview of professional traders and required a significant investment of time, money, and expertise. Today, there are more options for trading commodities.

Types of Commodities

1. Soft commodities: These are things that come from agriculture, such as wheat, coffee, chocolate, and animals.

2. Hard commodities are those that are produced from raw materials like metals, oil, and gas.

3. Energy Commodities: These include products like crude oil, natural gas, and electricity that are connected to the production and consumption of energy.

4. Financial Commodities: These are goods that include a financial element, such currencies, bonds, and interest rate futures.

5. Livestock Commodities: These are goods that come from livestock, such pork, beef, and poultry.

6. Agricultural Commodities: These are goods that are involved in the manufacture and distribution of agricultural goods including grains, fruits, and vegetables.

Commodities Market Trading

Participating in the spot or derivatives markets for commodities is often impossible for private investors. Direct access to these markets is typically only possible with a special brokerage account and/or particular credentials.

A young person can invest in the commodity market. However, every investment account they open must have a legal guardian co-sign it until they reach the age of majority in their country.

Along with possessing the necessary funds, they also need to be aware of the risks and potential advantages of investing in the commodities market. Before making an investment in any market, it is always advisable to speak with a financial professional.

Indirect access to commodities is available to average investors through the stock market itself.

As a result of the proliferation of exchange-traded funds (ETFs) that track various commodities or commodity indexes, the stock prices of mining and materials companies frequently exhibit a positive connection with commodity prices.

FAQs on Commodity Market

How can I learn about the current state of the commodity markets?

Online financial portals routinely discuss the pricing of various commodities, such as gold and crude oil. You may also get prices on the websites of commodities exchanges.

What Do Traders in Commodities Do?

Commodity traders buy and sell physical commodities (often known as "spot") or derivatives contracts that are based on physical commodities. Depending on the type of trader you are, you may use this market for a variety of purposes, including buying or selling actual items, hedging, speculation, or arbitrage.

Can I Make Money Investing in Commodities?

Commodities have risks and benefits, just like any other investment. An investor has to be knowledgeable about the markets for the product they want to trade, such as the possibility that oil prices might fluctuate based on the political climate in the Middle East. The kind of investment is crucial as well; ETFs offer more diversification and have lower risks than futures, which are riskier owing to margin requirements and more speculative. Gold in particular is seen to be a particularly effective hedge against inflation and a market downturn.

How Do Commodity Markets Function?

Buyers and sellers exchange cash in spot markets in exchange for rapid delivery of the physical item. In marketplaces for derivatives, buyers and sellers exchange money for the right to purchase products in the future. Before delivery may occur, holders of derivatives may roll over or liquidate their contracts. Counter-parties customize and trade over-the-counter forward contracts. Standardized contracts with stronger rules are used for exchange-listed futures and options.

What Kinds of Things Qualify as Commodities?

There are several goods available. Examples of energy goods include crude oil, natural gas, and gasoline. Precious metals include gold, silver, and platinum. Animals, wheat, maize, and soybeans are a few examples of agricultural goods. Additional items that you may trade include frozen orange juice, coffee, sugar, cotton, and others.

Chapter 10: Fomo Crypto

Cryptographer David Chaum first proposed the concept of digital money in the early 1980s, which is when cryptocurrencies first appeared on the scene.

With an emphasis on creating a safe method of online payment, Chaum finally developed a system known as DigiCash. To make sure that only the sender and receiver could see the transaction data, this system employed encryption.

The Cypherpunk movement started to take off in the 1990s. A group of computer scientists and cryptographers known as the Cypherpunks worked to develop a type of digital currency that was uncontrollable by banks or governments. Numerous technologies, notably the open-source project Bitcoin, were created by the Cypherpunks.

In 2009, the first Bitcoin was mined by an anonymous individual or group of individuals known as Satoshi Nakamoto.

Bitcoin is the first decentralized cryptocurrency, meaning that it does not rely on a central server or authority to verify transactions.

Bitcoin has gained popularity since it was first introduced and is currently the most popular cryptocurrency. As well as bitcoin, other cryptocurrencies including litecoin, ripple, and ethereum have been developed.

Since its start, the sector has advanced significantly, and cryptocurrencies are now an important component of the world's financial system. Despite its expansion, cryptocurrencies are still very volatile and are governed by various laws in different countries.

How Does Cryptocurrency Work?

Cryptocurrencies are a type of digital currency. It is created using shared and stored computer code on a blockchain, a form of online ledger.

Everybody may see a public record of all transactions that are stored on the blockchain. In order to keep transactions secure and anonymous, cryptocurrency uses encryption and cryptography.

It also lets users to send and receive money without the need for a bank or other third-party processor. Every transaction involving bitcoin is recorded on the blockchain. Every time a coin is sent, the blockchain is updated, and the transaction is recorded.

Types of Cryptocurrency

I'll mention a few of the thousands of cryptocurrencies that are allegedly created every day for various causes, but I encourage you to do your own research on each one as well.

1. Bitcoin (BTC): The first and most well-known cryptocurrency, Bitcoin is a decentralized digital currency that runs on a network of computers.

2. Ethereum (ETH): Ethereum is a free and open-source platform for building and deploying decentralized applications that is built on top of a blockchain.

3. Litecoin (LTC): Litecoin is a cryptocurrency that functions similarly to Bitcoin but with quicker and less expensive transactions.

4. Ripple (XRP): A digital payment network that enables swift and safe transactions, ripple (XRP) is one of them.

5. Dash (DASH): Dash is a cryptocurrency focused on privacy that aims to provide anonymous transactions.

6. Monero (XMR): Monero is a private and secure cryptocurrency with a decentralized and fungible emphasis.

7. Zcash (ZEC): Zcash is a cryptocurrency that focuses on privacy and is open source.

8. Dogecoin (DOGE): Based on the well-known "doge" meme, Dogecoin is a humorous cryptocurrency.

9. Stellar (XLM): Based on blockchain technology, Stellar is an open-source distributed payments network.

10. Tether (USDT): Backed by US dollars, Tether is a stablecoin that aims to keep its value constant.

Cryptocurrency Exchanges

Users may purchase, sell, or trade cryptocurrencies for other digital assets or fiat money like the US dollar on cryptocurrency exchanges, which are online marketplaces. Users can do direct business with one another through these exchanges without the assistance of a middleman.

Governments often regulate them, and in order to open an account and conduct transactions, users must disclose certain personal information. Exchanges for cryptocurrencies provide a range of services, including as margin trading, derivatives trading, and the ability to buy, sell, and trade digital assets. The costs for these services vary depending on the exchange.

Cryptocurrency Wallets

A digital wallet called a cryptocurrency is used to store, transfer, and receive digital currencies like Bitcoin, Ethereum, and Litecoin. The private and public keys that are required to approve transactions and access a user's bitcoin balance are kept in the wallet. Hot wallets, which are online, and cold wallets, which are offline and not online, are the two types of cryptocurrency wallets that are available.

How to Invest in Cryptocurrency

Step 1: Pick a cryptocurrency trading platform or service

Exchanges are a sensible option since they provide a variety of features and additional cryptocurrencies for trading, enabling users to withdraw money to their online wallets for safekeeping as well as enabling investors to purchase, trade, and retain bitcoin.

Exchanges for cryptocurrencies can take many different forms. Some exchanges enable users to stay anonymous, don't require personal information, and are decentralized.

Some populations, including refugees or those who live in countries with little to no infrastructure for government credit or banking, might benefit from anonymous transactions in order to better integrate into the mainstream economy.

Popular American exchanges are not decentralized and follow restrictions that require users to present identity documents. These exchanges include Coinbase, Kraken, Gemini, and Binance, and they give users access to Bitcoin and a growing number of other cryptocurrencies.

Step 2: Integrate Your Exchange with a Payment Method

Depending on the exchange, personal identification is required and may include pictures of a driver's license or Social Security card, as well as information about your job and financial resources. A standard brokerage account can be opened in a similar way.

Most exchangers let you instantly link your bank account, a debit or credit card, or both. Although you may use a credit card to purchase cryptocurrencies, the volatility in cryptocurrency pricing, when combined with the interest fees levied by the credit card, may raise the overall cost of purchasing a coin.

Despite the fact that cryptocurrencies like bitcoin are permitted in the US, certain banks may question or even block deposits to websites or exchanges that deal in cryptocurrencies. Additionally, exchanges charge a fee for each deposit made through a bank account, debit card, or credit card.

Step 3: Make a purchase

The functionality of cryptocurrency exchanges has increased to a level comparable to that of stock brokerages. Exchanges for cryptocurrencies offer a range of order types and investing choices. The majority of cryptocurrency exchanges let customers place market, limit, and sometimes even stop-loss orders.

Kraken provides the majority of order types, including as market, limit, stop-limit, take-profit, and take-profit limit orders.

Exchanges now provide ways for users to dollar-cost average into their chosen equities by setting up recurring investments. Customers may, for instance, arrange recurring transactions on Coinbase for every day, every week, or every month.

Step 4: Safekeeping

Cryptocurrency wallets, like those for bitcoin, enable you store digital assets more securely. When storing cryptocurrencies outside than on an exchange, such as in a personal wallet, investors continue to be the owners of the private key to their funds. Despite the fact that an exchange wallet is offered, it is not recommended for large or long-term bitcoin holdings.

Cryptocurrency Price Analysis

Cryptocurrency price analysis is the process of comparing the prices of different digital currencies to other assets in order to make an informed investment decision. This requires paying close attention to a variety of factors, including as market sentiment, news, technical indicators, and other data points, in order to obtain a sense of the future direction of a certain cryptocurrency.

By monitoring a coin's price over time and keeping an eye out for patterns and trends, investors may better understand a coin's movements and make more accurate predictions. Price analysis may also be used to evaluate the state of the market and identify potential points of entry for purchasing or selling coins.

Blockchain Technology

Blockchain technology establishes a decentralized digital ledger for keeping track of bitcoin transactions. It is a distributed ledger system that uses a network of computers to store and safeguard data. Each computer in the network keeps a record of every transaction that takes place, and the network as a whole shares these records.

The information stored on the blockchain is encrypted, connected, accessible, and secure. Blockchain technology enables secure, trustworthy, and efficient data management and storage. In addition to being used to validate and verify transactions, it may be utilized to create secure, immutable smart contracts.

Pros of Cryptocurrency Investing

1. Restricted Quantity: Because of the limited supply of cryptocurrencies, as demand grows over time, prices may rise.

2. Low Transaction Fees: Compared to traditional banking institutions, cryptocurrency transactions have far cheaper transaction fees.

3. Decentralized: Since there is no single entity in charge of cryptocurrencies, all transactions are private and safe.

4. High Liquidity: Because cryptocurrencies are so liquid, it is simple to trade them for other assets.

Cons of Cryptocurrency Investing

1. Volatility: Due to the high volatility of cryptocurrencies, values can change significantly in a short amount of time.

2. Security Risks: Hacking and frauds can result in huge losses when it comes to cryptocurrencies.

3. Regulatory Uncertainty: Since governments and central banks are still trying to determine how to regulate cryptocurrencies, investing in them is dangerous.

4. Lack of Adoption: The usage of cryptocurrencies is restricted by the fact that they are still not generally acknowledged as a means of payment.

Debunking Cryptocurrency Myths

Myth 1: Bitcoin is anonymous:

False. Since Bitcoin is a pseudonymous money, all of its transactions are permanently and publicly recorded on the blockchain. By withholding personal information, users can conceal their identity, but all Bitcoin transactions can be tracked.

Myth 2: Cryptocurrency is only used for illegal activities:

False. While cryptocurrencies may be used for illicit activities, they can also be utilized for things like investing, remittances, and purchasing products and services.

Myth 3: Cryptocurrency is too complicated to use:

False. Despite being a relatively new technology, Bitcoin is really extremely simple to use. A number of user-friendly exchanges and wallets are available that make it simple to purchase, exchange, and store cryptocurrencies.

Myth 4: All cryptocurrencies are the same:

False. Each cryptocurrency has a unique set of characteristics and application scenarios. Others are designed to make it easier to build decentralized apps or act as a store of wealth. Some are made to be used as payment systems.

Chapter 11: My Precious Collectibles

Since the beginning of recorded history, collectibles have existed. Ancient cultures frequently gathered artifacts with religious or historical importance, including coinage, ceramics, and jewelry. As a method to flaunt riches and authority, these things were frequently utilized as status symbols.

Rich households and collectors started accumulating things like books, manuscripts, artwork, and antiquities during the Middle Ages and the Renaissance. The objects were frequently viewed as a means of protecting a culture's history and legacy.

Numerous scientific and artistic innovations, including clocks, telescopes, and printing presses, were created during the Renaissance. The collections industry expanded as a result of these inventions and the artifacts that were acquired at this period.

In the 19th and 20th centuries, as trade and commerce expanded, collections became more and more well-liked. Mass-produced goods were now widely accessible and reasonably priced as a result of the industrial revolution. This resulted in the creation of certain collecting categories, like coins, stamps, and sports memorabilia.

Today, collectibles are becoming more and more popular. It is now simpler than ever to purchase and sell collectibles thanks to the growth of internet marketplaces. Collectors have access to a wide range of goods, including rare coins and vintage toys. Future collectibles may include an increasing number of goods as technology develops.

What is a Collectible?

A collectible is a product that, because of its rarity or popularity, is now worth far more than it did when it was first purchased.

The price of a particular collectible often depends on the availability of the item on the market as well as its overall condition.

Popular forms of collecting include those of stamps, coins, comic books, toys, and antiques. It takes a long time to amass a collection, and the items are usually kept safe from harm by their owners.

Understanding Collectibles

As was already said, collectibles are items that frequently sell for more money than they were originally worth. Many collectibles could command a high price if they're rare.

The state of a collectable has a significant impact on its price. If a collection is in pristine condition, its value could rise. However, there's a good chance that if something has deteriorated over time, it won't be worth anything at all.

Collectibles are neither as common nor a sensible investment as some marketers would have you believe. In the event that the product is still being produced, the company eventually recognizes the market signal and raises output to satisfy demand.

The store of value that characterizes a collectible doesn't enter the picture for the vast majority of products for many years or ever. After a production run is over, the amount of some commodities reduces via attrition, making them valuable due to their relative rarity.

New, mass-produced items that are currently on the market are occasionally referred to be collectibles. This is a marketing gimmick designed to raise consumer demand.

This is not the same phenomena that determines the price of genuine collectibles, though. There may be supply issues with items that are currently on sale, which raises the price that resellers want.

Types of Collectibles

1. Antique toys: Toys made before the 1950s are referred to as antique toys. Metal, wood, paper, and other materials can all be used to make these toys. Because of their scarcity and historical value, they are much sought for by collectors.

2. Coin Collecting: Collecting coins from different nations and historical periods is a passion. Coins can be gathered based on their design, minting site, nation of origin, or metal composition. Coin collectors frequently do research to find rare specimens and verify their worth.

3. Comic Books: Comic books are collections of panels and images that tell tales. They are frequently gathered for their distinctive artwork and tales. Rare issues, first printings, and autographed copies are frequently sought for by collectors for their collections.

4. Stamp Collecting: Collecting postage stamps from all around the world is the pastime of stamp collecting. Rare stamps, first-day covers, and mint stamps are frequently sought after by collectors for their collections.

5. Trading Cards: Also known as collectible cards, trading cards feature graphics and facts about a certain subject, such as sports, TV shows, or movies. For their collections, collectors frequently look for rare cards, signed cards, and limited edition cards.

<u>Examples of Collectibles</u>

Stamps and trading cards are two instances of genuine gems whose value has risen. One of the most costly collectibles ever created is the 1909 American

Tobacco Company T206 Honus Wagner baseball card. Cards of Honus Wagner, if in good condition, almost often sell for more than $1 million. In May 2021, the card brought in a new record price of $3.7 million.

It is a remarkable haul for a card that was offered as a free gift inside cigarette packs.

Another instance is The Treskilling Yellow. A Swedish postal stamp with an error that sold for over $2.3 million at auction in 2010.

Pop culture icons typically develop into collectibles with rising values. Today's valuables include stamps, baseball cards, and vintage comic books featuring the Fantastic Four, the Hulk, and Spider-Man.

You or your estate may be lucky since it is impossible to predict what the next million-dollar collectible will be, but don't depend on it to fund your retirement. However, feel free to hold on to the items that hold special importance for you.

Pros of Collectible Investing

1. Portfolio diversification: Collectibles may be a wonderful way to increase portfolio diversity. They can provide another possible source of returns and may be less erratic than equities and bonds.

2. Possibility of Appreciation: Over time, collectibles may gain value. The value of an object may rise when demand rises and supply falls for particular things.

3. Income Generating Potential: Rent or fees for using collectibles can be used to create income.

4. Potential Tax Benefits: Depending on the collectible's category, owning and selling the item may come with certain tax benefits.

Cons of Collectible Investing

1. Market Fluctuations: Collectibles are subject to market fluctuations, just like any other investment, and their value may decline over time.

2. Illiquidity: Many collectibles are difficult to exchange for cash, making them illiquid. In an emergency, this may make it challenging to immediately obtain money.

3. High Transaction Fees: The costs involved in purchasing and selling an item might vary greatly.

4. Expertise is Required: To succeed in investing in collectibles, a person needs have understanding of the items being bought. It may be challenging to obtain this.

FAQs on Collectibles

In what places may I sell my collectibles?

Thanks to internet markets, it is now simple to sell memorabilia. Along with the obvious eBay, you may also sell your treasures online on sites like Etsy, Craigslist, Facebook Marketplace, Bonanza, Ruby Lane, and ArtFire. Even Amazon, the biggest online retailer in the world, has a thriving collectibles sector. Local swap meetings, flea markets, and antique stores are face-to-face venues where you may sell your goods.

What Collectibles Are Popular at the Moment?

The demand for Pokémon trading cards has skyrocketed as of the summer of 2021. An untouched box of Pokémon cards from the late 1990s, which cost around $100 at the time, is now worth more than $50,000, according to a recent BBC study. Trading sports card sales were soaring in 2020, outpacing the S&P 500 in terms of growth.

How can I tell if a collectable is a wise financial decision?

To determine whether a collectible is a wise investment, you should do some research on the item to find out whether it has the potential to appreciate. Due to the fact that unusual goods often have greater growth potential, you should also take the item's rarity into account. Furthermore, it's important to stay educated about market conditions because they might affect how much a collectable is worth.

<u>Chapter 12: Market the Money</u>

Markets for short-term loans and investments are known as money markets.

Money markets have a long history that dates back to the early days of merchant banking, when companies need short-term funding to cover their transaction costs. "Call money" was the term for this kind of short-term lending, which was often just three months long.

In Amsterdam, the first structured money market was founded in 1609, and the Dutch East India Company rapidly used it as a major source of funding. In Amsterdam, there was a money market where businesspeople could lend money to one another at a set interest rate.

This gave them the resources they needed to pay for their travels to India and other far-off places.

The idea of money markets expanded throughout Europe and North America in the 18th century. Treasury bills, a type of short-term financial instrument that may be used as collateral for loans, were first issued by governments. Governments could borrow money safely and reliably using these treasury notes, and investors could buy them as a liquid asset.

Money markets started to enlarge more in the 19th century. Banks began issuing certificates of deposit (CDs), which investors could buy, as their own short-term debt instruments. The creation of these tools significantly facilitated enterprises' ability to acquire capital swiftly and affordably.

Money markets today play a significant role in the world financial system. They give investors a secure and accessible location to keep their money while also giving businesses the funding they require to develop and flourish.

In order to maintain low and steady interest rates, which contribute to an efficient and stable economy, money markets are also crucial.

What is Money Market?

A sort of financial market called the money market allows both individuals and companies to purchase and sell short-term investments. It works like a store where you may purchase and sell assets that will help you grow your money quickly. This differs from the stock market, where equities are bought and sold over a longer time frame. People may make their money work hard for them and earn a return on their investments by investing in the money market.

Types of Money Market Instruments

1. Treasury Bills - Treasury Bills (T-Bills) are short-term debt securities with a maturity of one year or less that are issued by the government. They don't pay interest and are sold at a discount from their face value.

2. Certificates of Deposit - Certificates of Deposit (CDs) are fixed-interest time deposits made with a bank or other financial institution for a certain length of time.

3. Commercial Paper - Issued by businesses to finance their ongoing operations, commercial paper (CP) is an unsecured, short-term financial instrument.

4. Repurchase agreements (Repos) are short-term contracts in which a seller consents to sell securities to a buyer in exchange for cash and consents to purchase the assets again at a higher price in the future.

5. Bankers' Acceptances - Bankers' Acceptances (BAs) are short-term debt instruments that banks issue and a third party accepts. The acceptance serves as the bank's assurance that the debt will be paid in full by the due date.

6. Eurodollar Deposits - Short-term deposits kept at banks outside of the United States are known as eurodollar deposits. Multinational firms frequently utilize them to finance their operations.

7. Federal Funds - Short-term loans between banks and other financial institutions are made with federal funds. The Federal Reserve sets the interest rate on the loans.

8. Money Market Mutual Funds are mutual funds that invest in a range of money market securities. They give investors a chance to earn rates that are greater than those offered by conventional bank accounts.

Pros of Money Market Investing

1. Low Risk: Money market investments are among the safest types of investments you can make. Due to the fact that money market assets are frequently guaranteed by the full confidence and credit of the United States government, default risk is normally low to nonexistent.

2. Liquidity: Investments in the money market are quite liquid, so you may frequently have access to your money within a day or two. They are therefore perfect for investors that want rapid access to funds.

3. Low Volatility: Investments in money markets often have lower volatility than other forms of assets, so you may anticipate fewer pronounced changes in the value of your investments.

Cons Money Market Investing

1. Low Returns: Investments in money markets often have relatively low returns that are frequently lower than the rate of inflation. You might not be able to keep up with the growing expense of living as a result of this.

2. Limited Access: Since authorized investors are often the only ones who can purchase money market investments, many people might not be able to benefit from them.

3. Lack of Diversification: Money market investments sometimes have a relatively narrow range of potential investments, which means they may not be as varied as other forms of investments.

FAQs on Money Market Investing

The Money Market: Is It Possible to Lose Money?
Most money market accounts are insured by the FDIC for depositors up to $250,000 per institution. Since money market instruments are so low risk, there is essentially little possibility that you will lose money if you own a CD or T-bill. At times of extreme financial stress, as as the height of the 2008 financial crisis, certain money market funds did "break the buck" and briefly incur losses, although this was quickly corrected.

What Justifies the Name "Money Market"?

The money market is the market for extremely safe and liquid short-term debt instruments. Because of these qualities, they are commonly seen as quick-exchangeable currency equivalents.

The Money Market: Why Is It Important?

Without a working money market, a modern financial economy cannot function successfully. As a result, capital is allocated to its most profitable use and savers are able to lend money to others who need rapid loans. These quick loans are necessary for governments, companies, and banks to take care of their urgent obligations or to meet legal criteria. They are typically prepared for a few days or weeks or even overnight. It also makes it possible for anyone with spare cash to earn interest.

Chapter 13: Manage Your Portfolio Youngsters

Congratulations!!! You have managed to go through the basics of investing, you've been exposed to various investing tips, and terms. You have achieved something great here today as there are many adults who have no idea about how to invest or simple basic terms.

Like in every field, theory is one part and execution is the other part, if you don't get your hands dirty in investing all you will have is just knowledge, you have to apply it. For every investment comes its own risk but there are many with little or no risk as stated above.

In this chapter, we will quickly take a look at ways you can manage your portfolio as a young investor, lets take a look at it now.

Too many young people rarely, if ever, make investments in their future. Many young people find it hard to understand a distant date that will happen in around 40 years.

But without investments to augment retirement income, if any, many incoming retirees will find it difficult to afford basic costs.

Particularly considering how much the economy will depend on freelance work, self-employment, and do-it-yourself financial planning. As fewer people work full-time, pensions are already extinct, and even plans with lower retirement security contributions are in decline.

However, you need to start investing when you're young. The earlier you begin, the more time your assets will have to mature. Here, we'll go through how to create a portfolio that will produce the best results and how to keep it that way.

Earlier the Better

Join a 401(k) retirement plan offered by your employer as soon as you begin employment to begin saving right away. Open an Individual Retirement Account (IRA) and designate a percentage of your earnings for a monthly contribution to the account if your employer does not provide a 401(k) plan. A quick and easy way to start saving money in an IRA or 401(k) is to set up an automatic monthly cash contribution (k).

It's important to keep in mind that interest and savings growth are only tax-free if the money is not withdrawn, therefore it's best to establish one of these retirement investment vehicles early in your working lifetime.

Early Allocation of a Riskier Asset

You are less likely to have big financial obligations as you age, such as a spouse, children, or a mortgage, to name a few, which is another reason to start saving early. Without these restrictions, you may allocate a small portion of your investment portfolio to riskier but more lucrative investments.

When you start investing when you're young, before your financial commitments start to pile up, you'll probably have more money available for investments and more time until retirement. If you have more money to invest for many years to come, you'll have a bigger nest egg for retirement.

An Exemplary Egg

To illustrate the benefit of starting early, imagine a person who starts investing $150 a month at the age of 25. At age 65, the retirement funds, assuming a 7% annual return on the invested capital, will be around $393,750. However, if the same individual starts setting aside $150 per month at age 35, their retirement savings would total around $183,750 by the time they are 65. There are certain tax benefits for individuals who start saving later, such as larger 401(k) contribution limits for those 50 and older and higher yearly contribution limits for IRAs.

Diversify

The objective is to select stocks from various market categories. Using an index fund is the simplest method to do this. Aim to invest mostly in safe, stable dividend-paying stocks with long-term growth potential, with a minor amount in riskier or higher-returning securities.

If you're investing in individual stocks, don't put more than 4% of your whole portfolio into any one stock. If one or more of your stocks see a fall using this strategy, your portfolio won't be adversely affected.

Bonds with AAA ratings are great long-term investments for both business and governmental issues. For instance, compared to short- and mid-term bonds, long-term U.S. Treasury bonds are safer and give a higher yield.

Maintain a low cost structure

Make investments with a cheap brokerage. Index funds might be considered when beginning to invest because of their low expenses. Since you intend to hold your investments for a long time, avoid routinely buying and selling in reaction to market fluctuations. By doing this, you might perhaps avoid financial losses in the event that the value of your stock declines as well as commissions and management costs.

Regular investing and self-control

Make sure you consistently and routinely invest in your assets. It might not be able to accomplish this if you lose your work, but after you find another one, maintain putting money into your portfolio.

Allocating assets and rebalancing

A specific percentage of your portfolio should be allocated to index funds, growth stocks, dividend-paying companies, and stocks with higher risk but better returns.

When your asset allocation shifts, rebalance your portfolio by raising or lowering your investment in each category to maintain the same percentage as when it was first created (market fluctuations affect the portion of your portfolio that is allocated to each category).

Tax Implications

A 401(k) or other tax-deferred account is a better place to build wealth than a tax-exempt one. But bear in mind that you must pay taxes on any withdrawals from tax-deferred retirement accounts.

When money is withdrawn from a Roth IRA, no taxes are required, but it can also grow tax-free.

To qualify for a Roth IRA, you must meet certain IRS requirements, such as having a modified adjusted gross income below a particular amount.

Your profits are federally tax-free if you have owned your Roth IRA for at least five years, are older than 5912 or younger than 5912, and the withdrawal is necessary due to your death, disability, first-time home purchase, or both.